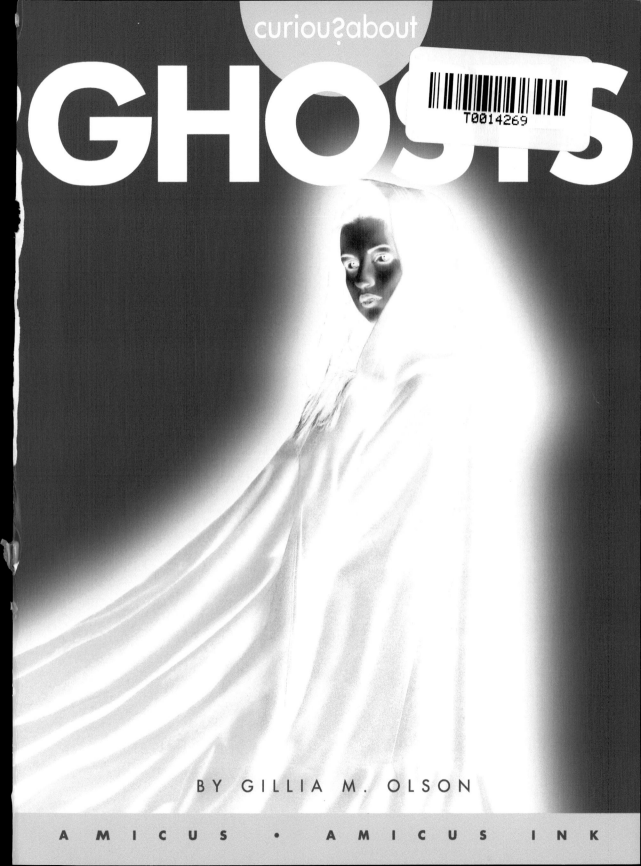

curious about

GHOSTS

BY GILLIA M. OLSON

AMICUS • AMICUS INK

T0014269

What are you

curious about?

CHAPTER **3** THREE

Looking for Proof

PAGE
18

Curious About is published
by Amicus and Amicus Ink
P.O. Box 227
Mankato, MN 56002
www.amicuspublishing.us

Copyright © 2022 Amicus.
International copyright reserved in all countries.
No part of this book may be reproduced in any
form without written permission from the publisher.

Editor: Alissa Thielges
Series Designer: Kathleen Petelinsek
Book Designers: Timothy Halldin & Ciara Beitlich
Photo researcher: Bridget Prehn

Library of Congress Cataloging-in-Publication Data
Names: Olson, Gillia M., author.
Title: Curious about ghosts / by Gillia M. Olson.
Description: Mankato, MN : Amicus, [2022] | Series: Curious
about unexplained mysteries | Includes bibliographical references
and index. | Audience: Ages 6–9 | Audience: Grades 2–3
Identifiers: LCCN 2019053100 (print) | LCCN 2019053101
(ebook) | ISBN 9781681519814 (library binding) | ISBN
9781681526287 (paperback) | ISBN 9781645490661 (pdf)
Subjects: LCSH: Ghosts—Juvenile literature. | Inquiry-based
learning—Juvenile literature.
Classification: LCC BF1461 .O854 2022 (print) | LCC BF1461
(ebook) | DDC 133.1—dc23
LC record available at https://lccn.loc.gov/2019053100
LC ebook record available at https://lccn.loc.gov/2019053101

Photos © iStock/captblack76 cover, 1; Shutterstock/Elena
Schweitzer 2 (left), 9; iStock/asbe 2 (right), 12; iStock/urbazon
3, 21 (top); Shutterstock/TukTuk Design 4 (person icons); iStock/
nevarpp 4–5; Deposit Photos/80sChild 6–7; Alamy/TopFoto 8;
iStock/johnnorth 11; Flickr/Terror on Tape 13; 123rf/Michal
Bednarek 14–15; Shutterstock/Mongkol Rujitham 17; 123rf/Lario
Tus 19; iStock/Suljo 21 (temp gun); Shutterstock/txking 21 (door);
Shutterstock/Lisa Turay 21 (dog); iStock/RobinOlimb 22, 23

Are ghosts real?

DID YOU KNOW?
**One in five people say they
have seen or felt a ghost.**

Are those ghosts, or
a trick of the mind?

That's the big question, isn't it? People have asked it for thousands of years. Half of people think ghosts are real. Is there scientific **proof**? Not yet. Still, people keep looking. Read on and see what you think.

What do ghosts look like?

Reports say ghosts can do things normal people can't, like float over water.

People say they've seen all kinds of ghosts. Some are see-through, floating people. Others look like fog. Still others look like shadows. It's good to check if your mind is playing a trick. Is that really a ghost? Or just a shadow of a tree?

DID YOU KNOW?

Some people say they've seen ghost dogs, cats, and even bears.

Famous picture of the Brown Lady of Raynham Hall

What color are ghosts?

Ghosts are known for what they wear. A "white lady" is a ghost in a flowing white dress. "Gray ladies" are in gray dresses. Scotland and Ireland have stories of ghosts in green dresses. They protect a home. The Brown Lady of Raynham Hall was named for her brown dress.

People sometimes think they see
white ladies in graveyards.

CHAPTER TWO

Are ghosts mean or nice?

That depends on the ghost! The Bell Witch was reported in 1817. The Bell family said the ghost pinched them and pulled their hair. In North Carolina, people have stories of the Gray Man. Before a hurricane, he will appear. He tells people to leave.

The Gray Man may warn people of a hurricane.

Can ghosts move things?

Some reports say ghosts can make things fly around.

Some might. **Poltergeist** means "noisy ghost." These ghosts are known to move things or make noise. Popper the Poltergeist is a well-known ghost. It appeared in the 1950s in New York. Things flew off shelves. Bottle tops popped off on their own. That's how the ghost got its name.

POLTERGEIST

"They're here."

DID YOU KNOW?
Popper's story was used in the movie Poltergeist in 1982.

Special camera effects can make a person look ghost-like.

Do ghosts show up in pictures?

People share lots of ghost pictures. Some might be real. Most are not. Ordinary things might seem like ghosts. Balls of light show up in pictures. They come from a camera's flash. It lights up a piece of dust or a bug. Other times, blurry pictures look like ghosts. It might just be a shaky camera.

Do ghosts give you nightmares?

About 8 percent of people have waking sleep paralysis in their lifetime.

8%

Not likely. But dreams can feel real. Sleep paralysis keeps you from acting out your dreams. Some people wake up while paralyzed. They aren't quite awake or asleep. They might see a ghost. It feels scary, but it's not real.

A ghost visit could just be part of your dream.

CHAPTER THREE

Where do ghosts live?

Anywhere. Ghosts are said to haunt the place they died. For example, there is a **hitchhiker** ghost. It is seen on the side of the road. A traveler might offer the ghost a ride. When they get to their stop, the ghost disappears. Later, the driver finds out the hitchhiker had died on the road!

A hitchhiker ghost may haunt
the place their car crashed.

How do ghost hunters look for ghosts?

Ghost hunters usually go to a place at night. They take pictures. They **record** video and sound. They ask the ghosts to make noise or turn lights on and off. They look for cold spots. Ghost hunters sometimes find things they can't explain. They keep looking. Maybe someday they will find real, solid proof of ghosts.

A spooky basement can be a perfect place to go ghost hunting.

SIGNS OF A GHOST

There is a cold spot. Ghost hunters use an infrared temperature gun.

Doors open and close on their own.

Pets act strangely toward you or empty spaces.

ASK MORE QUESTIONS

How do people fake ghost pictures?

What other places have ghosts been seen?

Try a BIG QUESTION:
If ghosts were proven real, how would that affect how people act?

SEARCH FOR ANSWERS

Search the library catalog or the Internet.
A librarian, teacher, or parent can help you.

Using Keywords
Find the looking glass.

Keywords are the most important words in your question.

?

If you want to know about:

- how to fake ghost pictures, type: FAKING GHOST PICTURES

- other places ghosts have been sighted, type: HAUNTED PLACES

FIND GOOD SOURCES

Here are some good, safe sources you can use in your research.
Your librarian can help you find more.

Books
Ghosts and Haunted Houses: Myth or Reality?
by Jane Bingham, 2019.

Searching for Ghosts
by Thomas Kingsley Troupe, 2021.

Internet Sites
Nat Geo Kids: How to Take Spooky Photos
https://kids.nationalgeographic.com/videos/photo-tips-with-hilary/#/778028611871
National Geographic is a respected source of journalism. It has profit and non-profit parts.

TedEd: Are Ghost Ships Real?
https://ed.ted.com/lessons/are-ghost-ships-real-peter-b-campbell
TED-ed is a non-profit educational site with videos on many topics.

Every effort has been made to ensure that these websites are appropriate for children. However, because of the nature of the Internet, it is impossible to guarantee that these sites will remain active indefinitely or that their contents will not be altered.

SHARE AND TAKE ACTION

Visit your local historical society.
Learn about the history of your town. Where do you think ghosts might be?

Look for tours of historic homes in your area.
There may even be spooky ghost tours for kids!

Are you feeling brave?
Ask a parent to go on a ghost hunt with you in your own home!

GLOSSARY

hitchhiker Someone on the roadside who asks for a ride from a stranger.

poltergeist A ghost that can make objects move.

proof Evidence.

record To store sound, images, or video so it can be heard or seen later.

report To give a spoken or written account of something one has seen, heard, or investigated.

sleep paralysis The state of not being able to move while dreaming; some people wake up while still paralyzed and may see things from their dreams.

INDEX

About the Author

Gillia M. Olson is a skeptic by nature but loves all things paranormal nonetheless. She stays curious and open-minded and hopes you will, too. She lives in southern Minnesota with her husband and daughter.